STEF SMITH

Stef Smith is a playwright whose work includes *Enough* (Traverse Theatre, Edinburgh); *Nora : A Doll's House* (Citizens Theatre, Glasgow; revived at Young Vic, London); *Girl in the Machine* (Traverse Theatre, Edinburgh); *Human Animals* (Royal Court Theatre, London); *Swallow* (Traverse Theatre); *Remote* (NT Connections); *Roadkill* (Edinburgh Festival Fringe).

Awards include the Olivier Award for Outstanding Achievement in an Affiliate Theatre, Critics Award for Theatre in Scotland for Best New Production, Amnesty International Expression of Freedom Award, Herald Angel Award, Total Theatre Award for Innovation, *The Scotsman* Fringe First Award (*Roadkill*); Scottish Arts Club Theatre Award for Drama, *The Scotsman* Fringe First Award (*Swallow*).

For screen, she has taken part in the BBC Drama Writers Room. Stef has also written two seasons of her the young adult series *Float* which was released on BBC iPlayer. It won a Royal Television Society Scotland award for Best Writer and Best Short Form Series at Series Mania in Lille.

GW00585185

AMY LIPTROT

Amy Liptrot is the author of two books, *The Outrun* and *The Instant*, both of which were *Sunday Times* bestsellers.

The Outrun was awarded both the Wainwright Prize in 2016 and the PEN Ackerley Prize in 2017. It was also a BBC Radio 4 Book of the Week, and has been translated into fifteen languages. A film of *The Outrun*, directed by Nora Fingscheidt and starring Saoirse Ronan, was released to wide acclaim in 2024.

The Instant was shortlisted for the Wainwright Prize for Nature Writing in 2022.

Amy writes columns and reviews for publications including the *Guardian* and *Caught by the River*. In 2021 she presented the BBC Radio 4 series *The New Anatomy of Melancholy*. Her work has also been included in the anthologies *Antlers of Water: Writing on the Nature and Environment of Scotland* and *Goodbye Europe*.

Stef Smith

THE OUTRUN

Based on the book by
Amy Liptrot

NICK HERN BOOKS

London
www.nickhernbooks.co.uk

A Nick Hern Book

The Outrun first published in Great Britain as a paperback original in 2024 by Nick Hern Books Limited, The Glasshouse, 49a Goldhawk Road, London, W12 8QP

The Outrun (original text) copyright © 2016 Amy Liptrot, published by Canongate Books Ltd

This stage adaptation of *The Outrun* copyright © 2024 Stef Smith

Amy Liptrot and Stef Smith have asserted their right, under the Copyright, Designs and Patents Act 1988, to be identified as the authors of this work.

Cover photography by Lawrence Winram

Designed and typeset by Nick Hern Books, London
Printed in Great Britain by Mimeo Ltd, Huntingdon, Cambridgeshire PE29 6XX

A CIP catalogue record for this book is available from the British Library

ISBN 978 1 83904 383 3

www.nickhernbooks.co.uk/environmental-policy

*Let me pull myself out of these waters. But they heap themselves
on me; they sweep me between their great shoulders; I am
turned; I am tumbled; I am stretched, among these long lights,
these long waves, these endless paths, with people pursuing,
pursuing.*

Virginia Woolf
The Waves

*I go through all this
Before you wake up
So I can feel happier
To be safe up here with you*

Björk
'*Hyperballad*'

The Outrun was co-produced by The Royal Lyceum Edinburgh and Edinburgh International Festival, and was first performed at the Church Hill Theatre as part of the Edinburgh International Festival on 31 July 2024. The cast and creative team were as follows:

WOMAN	Isis Hainsworth
DAD	Paul Brennen
BOY	Seamus Dillane
PERSON	Alison Fitzjohn
SCIENTIST	Reuben Joseph
FRIEND	Ros Watt
CHORUS	Tatiana Chater Davies
	Sally Georgina Pitts
	Lawrence Smith
	Rose Stachniewska
	Petre Dobre (D/deaf Artist
	for BSL performances)

Director	Vicky Featherstone
Composer	Luke Sutherland
Designer	Milla Clarke
Musical Director	Michael Henry
and Choral Arranger	
Movement Director and	Vicki Manderson
Intimacy Coordinator	
Lighting Designer	Lizzie Powell
Sound Designer	Kev Murray
Video Designer	Lewis den Hertog
Casting Director	Stuart Burt CDG
Costume Supervisor	Sophie Ferguson
Costume Assistant	Argyro Sapsouzidi
Associate Director	Vaila Anderson
Producer	David Dey
Production Manager	Grahame Coyle

Company Stage Manager	Dan Dixon
Deputy Stage Manager	Katy Steele
Assistant Stage Manager	Scott Ringan
LX Programmer	Neil Foulis
LX Supervisor	Roy Fairhead
AV Supervisor	Ellie Thompson
Sound No 1	Richard Bell
Sound No 2	Lana Kirk
Co-produced by	Edinburgh International Festival and Royal Lyceum Theatre Edinburgh

Acknowledgments

My sincere appreciation and gratitude to the cast, crew and creatives who were involved in the premiere production of *The Outrun*. It's been a privilege. And, also to the teams at the Lyceum and Edinburgh International Festival who made it possible. Especially David Greig whose idea sparked this project.

Special thanks to Luke Sutherland and Vicky Featherstone – I can't imagine going on this journey with anyone else. I've much to say but I'll keep it simple – I'm so grateful for your kindnesses, collaboration and sheer creativity. You're both so brilliant.

I'd also like to thank the following creatives for their generosity and talent in the development of this project: Moriah Austin-Brantly, Olatunji Ayofe, Tam Dean Burn, Jackie Crichton, Ewan Donald, Murray Fraser, Karen Fishwick, Ebenezer Gyau, Maia Journeau, John Kielty, Louise Ludgate, Cal Macaninch, Eve Nicol, Ben Presley, Cat Reilly, Dawn Sievewright and Frances Thorburn.

As ever, thank you to my agent Davina Shah and all those at TEAM. And my friends and family for their endless support and spare rooms. I'm glad I get to commit to print how much I love you all.

Finally, I'd like to thank Amy Liptrot. Without you and your beautiful book, this text wouldn't be here. Thank you for being up for the adventure.

S.S.

Characters

WOMAN
DAD
FRIEND
BOY
PERSON
SCIENTIST

Notes

A dash (–) as the character prefix denotes words spoken by a chorus or a single chorus member. These words can be divided however the production sees fit.

A forward slash (/) denotes an interruption.

This play is best understood as a piece of music which swells and bursts, like waves crashing on a shore.

There are few stage directions, imagine it as you wish.

This text went to press before the end of rehearsals and so may differ slightly from the play as performed.

–   From the north-east coast of Scotland.
It's seven miles away as the crow flies.

Across the Pentland Firth
To an ensemble of seventy islands.
Collectively called – Orkney.

Ancient and animal.
Cliffs and corncrakes.
Wave power and progress.

We cross –
With seals.
And waves.
And killer whales.

We cross –
With heartache.
And hope.
And killer whales.

We cross –
With myths.
And truths.
And killer whales.

We cross the Pentland Firth
To an ensemble of seventy islands.
Collectively called – Orkney.

Where a helicopter lands in a storm.
And a baby girl is placed on her father's lap.

He sits sedated and straightjacketed, soon to
be sectioned.
Bipolar and hospital-bound.

Bright pink, premature and hours old, the
baby girl just curls into her blanket.

The baby girl just...

And her father's mouth moves but what is said is lost to the wind, to the noise of an engine.

Is slipped into the inconsistency of memory.

As Mother and Daughter are taken in a different direction to Father, it's tough to tell the difference between sea spray and tears.

Years pass.

Seasons cycle.

The coastline erodes.

A body stretches out.

A premature baby to a toddler to a pre-teen to a young woman.

Who stands with exam results in her hands.

It's been eighteen years of tough and tumble. A bi-polar dad, a born-again Christian mum.

Ups and downs like a gull riding the gusts.

Like a gull riding the gusts.

WOMAN Eighteen years on this farm. And increasingly it feels like a collection of fields on the edge of the earth.

The Outrun is the largest field on the farm. It stretches along the coastline where the grass is always short from wind and sea spray. There are no walls here and in the early years sheep used to fall off the cliff. But now – due to breeding – they've learnt not to fall but to dodge the edges. Their genetics ensuring their survival.

It's my favourite place to sit. Amongst the wind and wool. On the edge of the earth.

And it's where your mobile phone gets the best signal.

The ding of a text message arriving. She looks at her phone.

In a static caravan. Her dad is rolling a cigarette.

The woman walks in, holding her exam results.

He looks up. She smiles. Shows him.

DAD   Good results. Though it was never in doubt.

                Edinburgh, then. Is it?

WOMAN   Yeah.

DAD   English, is it?

WOMAN   English Literature. Yeah.

                He simply nods. Neither of them mind the silence.

DAD   Smart girl.

                You get that from your mother.

WOMAN   I get it from you both.

DAD   Have you told her?

WOMAN   Not yet.

DAD   I think she is back at the house.

                She'll be pleased for you.

WOMAN   Not as pleased to see that you've cleaned this caravan.

DAD   Even I know it needed it.

                Silence.

                Did you feel anything out there?

WOMAN	What?
DAD	Did you feel anything out there?
WOMAN	No.
DAD	I felt those tremors. They're back again.
	People think it's jets. But it's not aeroplanes, it's never the navy ships either. It's the caves... caves under the earth, water gets trapped and compresses the air at a high pressure so /
WOMAN	as the water retreats the air bubble explodes causing a boom.
DAD	A boom.
	Yes.
	Or what is it you told me? The Stoor Worm. Maybe it is that. What was it? A snake?
WOMAN	A beast. With a head as big as a mountain. It was killed by being cooked from the inside. As it died its teeth fell out to make these islands. So, the story goes.
DAD	A terrible way to go, being cooked from the inside.
WOMAN	I imagine so.
DAD	You used to like all those stories, folk stories.
WOMAN	Still do.
	Silence.
DAD	What?
WOMAN	You don't usually talk about stories.
	DAD *shrugs.*
DAD	Maybe today I feel like talking about stories.

Don't worry I'm not... I'm fine. I'm not... you know.

Silence.

One of the ewes was limping earlier, I need to go and check on her. If you go into town, get more tobacco. There is only enough left for one more.

WOMAN   Do you not want help?

DAD   You can help if you want.

He begins to get ready to go out.

I put your notebook and things on the side. Almost spilt my coffee over it while I was shuffling things about.

Do you write about me in those things?

WOMAN   I write about me. And you. And here.

DAD   D'you think they'll ever run out of things to write about Orkney?

WOMAN   Doubt it.

DAD   It all tends to be a bit misty-eyed and romantic wouldn't you say. There is not much written about the sheep shit and storms.

WOMAN   Don't pretend you want to be anywhere else.

Silence.

DAD   And don't you forget the tobacco.

DAD *leaves.*

WOMAN   And despite him, or because of him, I write down everything anyone ever told me about this place. I litter my journal with facts and figures and the stories that shaped these islands. The declining population after World War Two, the loss of its importance in trading routes, how it's closer to the Artic Circle than London. And how sometimes all this space can feel – suffocating.

FRIEND   Do you want another?

WOMAN   What did you say?

FRIEND   D'you want another?

WOMAN   Yes. Please.

He passes her a bottle of something.

FRIEND   So, you're just going to fuck off into the big bad world?

WOMAN   Something like that.

FRIEND   Fair play I suppose. My dad said it's only oil money now, on the island, 'money in oil' like it's his fucking catchphrase. But it's not our money is it. All that oil money ends up somewhere else. Doesn't end up here.

WOMAN   Some of it ends up here.

FRIEND   Aye, but not enough.

WOMAN   It's not that simple.

FRIEND   Said like a southerner.

WOMAN   I was born here.

FRIEND   If your folks aren't from here, you're not from here.

WOMAN   By that logic that means you're not from here.

FRIEND   Orkney is a place where people just wash up.

WOMAN	That's what happens when most of your country is coast.
FRIEND	You'll hate Edinburgh. Too many people and too many buildings.
WOMAN	And you're jealous.
	Silence.
FRIEND	Give me one good reason to go live there?
WOMAN	Shops. Gigs. And finally some fucking glamour.
FRIEND	Oh, aye and just last week you were busy saying that this is the best place on earth.
WOMAN	Who gives a shit what I say.
FRIEND	I do.
WOMAN	Don't do that.
FRIEND	What?
WOMAN	Get sentimental. I hate that.
	Silence.
FRIEND	Aren't you a wee bit – you know… about leaving.
WOMAN	Scared?
	No way.
	Aren't you scared about staying?
	Silence.
FRIEND	Want to take this wine up the ruins? All the tourists will have left by now.
WOMAN	And there, planted there like it is our playground are the Neolithic Stones, thousands of years old. Watching us get wasted, bottle after bottle, shitfaced, singing

and staggering and the wind whirls around
us, playful and pissed. The wine and
wooziness comes like waves, hitting against
the soil, hitting against my skin. The line
blurs between the land and my lungs and
the airstream and alcohol, wounded and
wonderful, my body is made of oceans. And
earth. And ancient Gods.

–   Oceans.
            And earth.
            And ancient Gods.

            Oceans.
            And earth.
            And ancient Gods.

            Oceans.
            And earth.
            And ancient Gods.

WOMAN   Edinburgh is – everything. Four years
            of freedom. A degree done in a daze of
            Smirnoff and sex and sometimes, even,
            studying. My life becomes bigger than
            I can hold. Arthur's Seat. Princes Street.
            The waters of Leith. Taking it all in. Like
            a basking shark. Consuming. Consuming.

–   Consuming. Consuming.

            Taking it all. Like a basking shark.
            Consuming.
            Taking it all in. Consuming. Consuming.

WOMAN   And then – it's done.

            And it's back... to Orkney.

            And as soon as I get there I send text
            messages to friends in the city. SMSs like
            SOSs. An anchor into an old life.

            Silence.

FRIEND	Thought about visiting you in Edinburgh. But I've been busy.
WOMAN	Doing what?
FRIEND	Stuff.
WOMAN	Oh right. Stuff?
FRIEND	We all didn't just stand still because you left the island.
WOMAN	I know that I just…
FRIEND	I've been working. And helping my mum do up house and… I've started seeing someone.
WOMAN	Seeing someone. Who?
FRIEND	You wouldn't know her.
WOMAN	How would I not know her?
FRIEND	She just moved here. Got a job at the hotel.
WOMAN	Must be hard. To come here from somewhere else.
FRIEND	Aye, well she likes it. She's gonna stay if they keep her on after the season ends. She said she likes living by the sea.
	Silence.
WOMAN	I always thought it was strange how in the centre of Edinburgh there were sea gulls. Edinburgh is miles from the sea. But they would be there, eating out of bins. I didn't understand why they wouldn't rather stay by the sea. It's fresher… life is fresher by the sea, on the edge.
FRIEND	It's just a bird.
WOMAN	Maybe.

FRIEND	You look different.
WOMAN	How?
FRIEND	Dunno. Just different.
	They stopped selling those magazines you like – those fashion ones.
WOMAN	It's because I had to get them ordered in.
FRIEND	I flicked through one after you left but I got bored, the whole thing was like one big advert. I find it hard to appreciate a picture that doesn't have a hill in it.
WOMAN	You're becoming your dad.
FRIEND	And you're becoming yours.
	Silence.
	Sorry about your folks. Did you see it coming?
WOMAN	The divorce? No.
	But maybe it's surprising that they could stay together so long.
FRIEND	Aye. A strange mix.
	Sorry.
WOMAN	She's moved into town. He is still on the farm.
FRIEND	It's good you're staying with him
	Your old man is as much that farm as the fences.
WOMAN	He likes the quiet.
FRIEND	Do you think you'll stay? Or go back to Edinburgh?
	Silence.

WOMAN   I'm going to try staying.

Just for a bit, at least.

D'you know of any jobs going free?

FRIEND   What are you willing to do?

WOMAN   Anything... maybe I could come and work with you.

FRIEND   On the oil terminal? You ever been a cleaner before?

WOMAN   No. But I'll give it a shot.

FRIEND   I thought you wanted to be a journalist.

WOMAN   I just need something while I figure it all out.

Please.

FRIEND   It's long days and hard work.

WOMAN   But good pay and plenty of shifts?

Silence.

FRIEND   If I'm vouching for you /

WOMAN   I promise I'll be the best cleaner you've ever had.

FRIEND   And it means I'll technically be your manager.

WOMAN   Perfect. You won't need to worry about me.

I'll fit right in.

FRIEND   There are all sorts there. You can see from their rooms. A real muddle of folk.

WOMAN   Sounds good.

Silence.

FRIEND   Alright.

WOMAN   I work hard at working hard. My hands grow rough, but the pay packets keep me ploughing on.

The commute in the morning to get the ferry is the best thing about the job. Usually done at dawn to drum and bass.

I can see myself get increasingly shit at the job but I can't bring myself to care. A degree left to decay. And instead, I become an expert in dirt and drinking and digital SOSs

Calling out over landscapes and landlines

Calling out into caves

Feeling the boom of compressed cries.

Feeling the...

–   Returning. Repeating. Reliving. Refining.

Returning. Repeating. Reliving.

Returning. Repeating.

FRIEND   Why have you only cleaned one room?

You know the other girls are complaining about picking up your work.

Silence.

Are you hung over again because...

Silence.

Have you been...

You know it's only been a few months and I've found you crying more times than I...

I should have known better than to hire a friend because it's... it's not working out.

Silence.

I'll give you next month's pay... and then...
I'm asking... telling you.... go find another
job. You're not happy here.

WOMAN   Leaving work feels like wire wool across
a wound. But I pack a rucksack and buy
a one-way ticket to London. I walk into
each of the rooms in the farmhouse and
say – goodbye. Goodbye. Goodbye.

I get the ferry down to Aberdeen and then
the train from Aberdeen to London. I do it
in one forward motion, like a gull on the
gusts. It takes over twenty hours from door
to door. I turn up at my new room, open
a beer and begin again.

–   Expanding. Consuming.
Like a basking shark.
Consuming.

WOMAN   I am an animal let out of captivity, free to
run in this new land with new things and
people to fall in love with. I take baths at
six a.m., cut my hair, wear strange dresses,
apply for jobs, do drugs and drink. My body
feels amazing. Oceans. And earth. And
ancient Gods.

–   Taxis. The Tube. Train lines.
Expanding outward.
With too much to taste. To touch. To take in.
Too much. In love with the too-muchness of
it. In love.

WOMAN   I begin a blog. I want to write this all down.
The days pass, as the word count goes up.
Thousands of words, minutes, moments.

Expanding outward into the internet.
Connecting to people I've never met. And
I take them with me. Through the city.

BOY	I don't think they can really call this a picnic – there is no food.
WOMAN	Not true. Someone had a bag of crisps about two hours ago.
BOY	You're not from here.
WOMAN	No.
BOY	Scottish?
WOMAN	Sure. Why not.
BOY	What brings you to London, then?
WOMAN	I want to write.
BOY	Write about what?
WOMAN	Anything that is interesting.
BOY	Anything is interesting if you look at it the right way.
	I think you're pretty interesting. Enigmatic. Is that the right word?
WOMAN	How should I know? People aren't very good at describing themselves. They soften all the edges.
BOY	And people like to be at the centre of their own stories.
WOMAN	What does even that mean?
BOY	Fuck knows. It's just something I read on the internet.
	WOMAN *playfully hits* BOY.
	Hey.
WOMAN	I have a feeling you're full of bullshit.
BOY	But it's very friendly bullshit. Alluring almost, you could say.
WOMAN	Alluring.

BOY	Okay, you're right. People aren't very good at describing themselves.
WOMAN	I'd say you're – somewhat – alluring.
BOY	'Somewhat.' Tough crowd.
WOMAN	I'm just being honest.
BOY	Well. I appreciate that. I guess.

Silence. Flirtation.

It suits you, London.

WOMAN	You don't know me.
BOY	I'd like to get to know you.
WOMAN	'I'd like to get to know you?'… what sort of line is that?

She pushes him away. BOY *shrugs. Comes closer again.*

In silence, BOY *and* WOMAN *look at each other.*

D'you know why I really moved here?

BOY *shakes his head.*

Because I want to experience – everything.

BOY	Everything?
WOMAN	Everything.
BOY	Sounds exhausting.
WOMAN	I think it sounds exciting.
BOY	I think you sound drunk.
WOMAN	Most people are more interesting when they are drunk.
BOY	Or maybe you just find them more interesting once you've had a drink?
WOMAN	Probably.

BOY	I like your eyes.
WOMAN	Thank you.
	I like your socks.
BOY	Thank you.
	Silence.
WOMAN	Do you like dancing?
BOY	… yeah. I like dancing.
WOMAN	Yeah.
BOY	Yeah.
WOMAN	Yes.
BOY	Yes.
WOMAN	And in a warehouse, west of somewhere from the Central Line, it's waves of wine and bodies and booze. Dancing and dreaming. Dissolving into drugs. Dancing to feel alive and afloat and amazing and animated, like this can never end. It won't end. London is all limbs and light.
–	Limbs and light. Ancient and animal. Bodies and booze. Limbs and light. Ancient and animal. Bodies and booze.
BOY	It's big.
WOMAN	Yeah. We rent the whole house.
BOY	How many of you live here?
WOMAN	Lots of us. Just as I remember someone's name they leave. But my room gets all the sunlight and there is always someone to talk to. If I want to talk to someone that is.

BOY	They say everyone in London is looking either for work, a room or a lover.
WOMAN	Which are you looking for?
BOY	Well. I've got a room. And a job.
	So.
	Silence.
	They kiss.
WOMAN	We text each other constantly, rush to meet each other at the end of the day. I wrap my legs around him, like a life raft.
	And there is a tenderness to him that I... well... it just...
BOY	Why are you smiling like that?
WOMAN	Like what?
BOY	Like that.
WOMAN	I just think... this is it.
BOY	What?
WOMAN	I think this is it.
	This is where I belong.
	Here with you.
	Don't you think?
BOY	I think you're not like anyone I've ever met.
WOMAN	Can I live with you?
BOY	What?
WOMAN	What?
BOY	It's only been six months.
WOMAN	I know.
	And I know this it is.

BOY	Then, yes. I want you to live with me. I'd love that.
WOMAN	And I love you.
	Silence.
BOY	And I love you.
	They kiss. Passion. Tenderness.
WOMAN	To be held.
	Is like exhaling.
	I love him so much that I almost can't…
–	To be held.
	Is like exhaling.
	To be held.
BOY	You look nice.
WOMAN	I feel nice.
BOY	Have you been writing?
WOMAN	A little.
	It's hard after a day in that office. The air is so… thick. Even the plants are dying. I thought it was literally impossible to kill a cactus.
BOY	I know temping is shit but /
WOMAN	Can we go out?
BOY	Where?
WOMAN	Just – out.
	Are you coming?
BOY	Sure.
WOMAN	Then make mine a double.

BOY   Where are you going?

WOMAN   Out.

                Are you coming?

BOY   Sure.

WOMAN   Then make mine a double.

BOY   Where are you going?

WOMAN   Out.

                Are you coming?

BOY   Sure.

WOMAN   Then make mine a double.

BOY   Where are you going?

WOMAN   Out.

                Are you coming?

BOY   Sure.

WOMAN   Then make mine a double.

BOY   Where are you going?

WOMAN   Out.

                Are you coming?

BOY   No, not tonight. I'm knackered.

WOMAN   The curser on my computer blinks. And I
                am trying to write about last night. I ended
                up in some club with all these goths and
                they were so surprisingly kind and lovely
                and then – I can't remember. I woke up
                wearing earrings I don't own. The gasps
                of forgetting are becoming gaps. They
                are becoming... gullies. But still, I keep
                writing. And people keep reading.

BOY   Where are you going?

WOMAN	Out.
	Are you coming?
BOY	No.
WOMAN	Then make mine a double.
BOY	Where are you going?
WOMAN	Out.
	Are you coming?
BOY	No.
WOMAN	Then make mine a double.
BOY	Where are you going?
WOMAN	Out.
	Are you coming?
BOY	Where are you going?
WOMAN	Out.
BOY	Where are you going?
WOMAN	Out.
BOY	Where are you going?
WOMAN	Out.
	Out.
	Out.
BOY	Enough.
	I've got work tomorrow.
WOMAN	So, do I.
BOY	Yeah, but /
WOMAN	But temping is not as important as your work?
BOY	I thought you wanted to write.
WOMAN	I write.

BOY   Internet posts about being drunk aren't
               really writing.

WOMAN   I don't need you to judge, thank you. You
               drink as much as me.

BOY   No, I don't.

               Silence.

               Maybe we could both cut down?

WOMAN   I'll cut down – as soon as it's a problem.
               And it's not a problem.

BOY   If you say so.

WOMAN   And I do say so.

               And I leave the pub early to go home, alone.
               Because at home I can drink at a faster rate
               than I can get served. Because... I want it.
               Because tonight, I want alcohol more than
               my friends.

               Even though the gaps are getting...

               One moment I am here and the next I am...

               And the curser on my computer is blinking
               at me.

               The word count staggers up. People read.
               People watch.

               The repeating. But not remembering.

               Repeating but not...

–   Gaps. Gasps.
               Out. Out. Out.
               Gaps. Gasps.
               Out. Out. Out.

BOY   What the fuck were you thinking?

WOMAN   Don't shout at me.

BOY   What the fuck were you thinking?

WOMAN	Don't shout at me.
BOY	It's dark and you're drunk, and you took your bike up that towpath.
WOMAN	I wanted to see the sunrise from Hampstead Heath.
BOY	You could have died.
WOMAN	But I didn't.
BOY	That doesn't make it okay.
WOMAN	Can you not…

Silence.

BOY	Do you think you've broken anything?
WOMAN	No. I just scratched myself getting out of the canal.
	I lost a shoe.
	And my diary is soaked.
BOY	I'll put it on the radiator along with your… shoe.
	This is getting tiring.
	All these tears. All these accidents.
	It's tiring.
WOMAN	Can you just hold me?
	Please.

He chooses not to hold her.

BOY	I'll run you a bath.
WOMAN	I pour myself a glass of wine and drink it in one motion. I turn my music up and, on my phone I look at images of Orkney, and I pour another drink, and another, bleeding and bruised… I pour another drink. I begin to write but…

I begin to write but…

I just end up dreaming… of oceans. And earth. And ancient Gods.

BOY   You're drunk?

I thought we were going out for dinner.

It's the first plan just me and you in…

I thought…

Silence.

WOMAN   You know you look handsome in this light.

BOY   Stop.

WOMAN   Something about how your hair just /

BOY   Stop.

WOMAN   Don't you want to /

BOY   Stop.

Stop.

Silence.

I can't.

I can't do this any more.

Your drinking is destroying you.

And me. And us.

We haven't had actual sex in weeks and weeks.

WOMAN   I've just been…

BOY   Busy?

Silence.

I can't do this.

WOMAN   No.

BOY	I can't.
WOMAN	No.
BOY	I can't.
WOMAN	Don't leave.
	Please.
	Silence.
BOY	I know you pretend the first drink I see in your hand is your first – but it's not. I hear you sneak out, I find bottles, I'm bored of picking you up off the floor. We are too young for this bullshit.
WOMAN	Please.
	Silence.
	I need you.
BOY	I know.
	Silence.
WOMAN	I drink because it all... feels overwhelming.
BOY	I know.
	Silence.
	But plenty of people are overwhelmed. And they don't drink like this.
WOMAN	But I...
	Silence.
	Please.
	Don't leave.
	Please.
	Because it's just you left.
	I don't really have any other...
	And I can't seem to...

I can't... find my way back.

Silence.

BOY   I've been telling you to get help. For
                months. I've sent links and given you
                leaflets. And you've done nothing but sit
                and get pissed. So, if you really want help –
                go get help.

WOMAN   But I can't... I don't know how.

BOY   Then find a way. Because I've done all
                I can.

                And I'm not having you waste my life along
                with your own.

                Silence.

WOMAN   Please. Please. Don't leave.

                I love you.

                I love you so much I...

BOY   And I love you.

                That's what makes this so fucking shit.

                But right now, there is only space for you.
                I could be anyone. I'm just someone you
                sleep next to in bed – that's when you sleep
                in bed.

                I'm sorry.

                I'm... sorry.

                Silence.

WOMAN   And it's early or late... I open my window
                to sit and smoke. Streetlights shine and
                the sound of karaoke strikes and just for a
                second, I see a fox. Stalking the shadows,
                beautifully. The fox stares at me... the two
                of us... strangers in a strange land.

Torn pages. Half-finished thoughts. Photos on my phone of places I don't remember. Bruises arrive like bad magic tricks. Ta-dah. The vanishing lady. One moment she is there and the next... ta-dah.

A vanishing life. Shrinking and shrivelling with every sip.

They are on the phone.

DAD   It's late to be calling.

            I said it's late to be calling.

WOMAN   I was just... I just... I was just calling to ask...

            About the lambs. How many this year?

DAD   We're up to fifteen. Still plenty to come.

WOMAN   Still plenty to come.

DAD   I know it's your favourite time of year.

WOMAN   Yeah.

            Yeah.

            It's my favourite time of year.

DAD   Was that it?

WOMAN   Yeah.

            Yeah.

            That's... it.

            Silence.

DAD   Call in a few days, will you?

            Silence.

            I'll tell you the new numbers then.

            Bye, now.

WOMAN   Ten different houses in five years. My
               belongings live in friends' attics and
               garages. I travel light so that no one notices
               when I just – disappear.

               In this new shithole that I call home, I sit
               on the sofa, and hear scrapes and scratches
               above me. The landlord sends someone to
               check it out, and it turns out there is a space
               in the attic, just above my head, where
               pigeons have been flying in and becoming
               trapped. Just above my head, a pile of dead
               pigeons are rotting.

–   Rotting. Returning. Repeating.
               Reliving. Refining. Rotting.
               Rotting. Returning. Repeating.
               Reliving. Refining. Rotting.

BOY   How did you find my address?

               It's not okay just to turn up.

               You're not welcome here.

               Please. Leave.

               I'm asking you to leave.

               How did you find my address?

               It's not okay just to turn up.

               You're not welcome here.

               Please. Leave.

               I'm asking you to leave.

               How did you find my address?

               It's not okay just to turn up.

               You're not welcome here.

               Please. Leave.

               I'm asking you to leave.

WOMAN	But.
BOY	I'll call the police if you don't leave.
WOMAN	I keep having these seizures, that arrive earlier and earlier into drinking. They begin with a tension in my wrists. Then my elbows freeze, and I can't seem to... I just can't seem to...

I'm sleepwalking into seizures. And is no more writing. There is no more watching. There is – nothing.

I wish I had the guts just to give up.

Silence.

It's the dead of the night when a stranger's car stops and offers me a lift, a drink and a distraction. We drive through the city, barely chatting. He is silhouetted by the streetlights when without warning he punches me in the face.

He hits me again and... I'm bleeding.

Be quiet. He says to me. Be quiet.

And he tears at my tights. Be quiet.

But I am not quiet.

I scream. I scream – I am stronger than you, I am stronger than you. I am stronger than you.

–	I am stronger than you. I am. I am. I am.
WOMAN	I am taken to the hospital. X-rayed and weighed, and I am lighter than when I was teenager. Dressed in a green medical gown, my head is stitched from where he hit me.

And I go to the bathroom, I look at myself in the mirror.

I look at myself and…

Who is that woman…

Silence.

As I sit with the police. I just know…

I know my body needs a break. Just for a little while… just a little…

Silence.

My first attempt at not drinking lasts four weeks. I take a medication which provokes an allergic response to alcohol. It doesn't work.

Three attempts at sobriety, and there is an – emptiness. I've lost booze and I am desperately searching for what I need to fill me up.

Coffee, sex, love, new clothes, the internet. Sometimes I crave the next cigarette when I've just started smoking one.

–   Coffee, sex, love, new clothes, the internet. Sometimes I crave the next cigarette when I've just started smoking one. Coffee, sex, love, new clothes.

WOMAN   I try to write but…

–   Coffee, sex, love, new clothes, the internet.

WOMAN   I am just a girl from an island who has woken up in London twelve years later to find herself in a church hall with a group of misfits, drinking tea from chipped mugs. I am finally granted a place in outpatient rehab. Where saying 'cheers' instead of thanks was triggering territory.

PERSON   What's your story then?

Silence.

Everyone else is sharing.

Silence.

It's rude just to rely on everyone else.

Silence.

WOMAN   Three months. Four days a week. For six hours.

Stories of shitting the bed. Smoking. Shooting up. Surviving. Sex-work. Families falling apart. Detoxes. Depression. Jail. Jaundice.

PERSON   I wish they let us have coffee... but apparently it counts as a stimulant. You're young – for this.

–   Three months. Four days a week. For six hours.

Stories of shitting the bed. Smoking. Shooting up. Surviving. Sex-work. Families falling apart. Detoxes. Depression. Jail. Jaundice.

Three months. Four days a week. For six hours.

Three months. Four days a week. For six hours.

Silence.

PERSON   This your first time at rehab?

WOMAN   Yeah. You?

PERSON   Oh, no. Fifth try is a charm – right?

I was clean fourteen months last time. Relapsed, went on a bender, ended up spending five days in a psychiatric ward. This time I lost a tooth. Last time I lost my husband. But here I am.

WOMAN   Here we are.

PERSON   Ironic isn't it, that we don't stop talking about the very thing we are all trying to kick. I talk more about drink and drugs now I'm sober than when I was getting shit-faced. You should start talking in the group. You've got weeks more of this – tediousness.

–   Three months. Four days a week. For six hours.

               Stories of shitting the bed. Smoking. Shooting up. Surviving. Sex-work. Families falling apart. Detoxes. Depression. Jail. Jaundice.

PERSON   You know I had a cousin from Elgin, are you from up there?

               Silence.

WOMAN   I don't want to get it wrong.

PERSON   What?

WOMAN   I worry about talking here because… I've spent so long messing up and covering up and apologising… I worry I'll get it wrong.

PERSON   Trust me, whatever you've done. Someone here will have done worse.

WOMAN   Three months. Four Days a Week. For six hours. The rest of the time… all those other hours… the curser on my computer just blinks at me. It's the only thing watching.

               Blinking. Blinking. Blinking.

               Silence.

PERSON   Sleeping is hard, isn't it. Without a little something. I barely get more than a few hours a night.

WOMAN	In my dreams I am drinking.
PERSON	That takes a while to leave.
WOMAN	Do you think everyone here tells the truth?
PERSON	Well. Addicts aren't known for their truth-telling. And we certainly tell our stories over and over. I imagine they become...
WOMAN	Refined. By repeating.
PERSON	Something like that.
	Everyone certainly smudges together after a while, don't they? Especially with a drink in you.
WOMAN	Do you think we are all just the same?
PERSON	Addicts? Yes.
	And no.
	I think we are just like everyone else.
	And how awful is that.
	How wonderful is that.
	Silence.
WOMAN	I came to London because I wanted to experience everything, but it has left me with nothing.
PERSON	I'm sorry.
WOMAN	Don't be. I've done this to myself.
PERSON	Doesn't mean I can't be sorry.
	Silence.
WOMAN	Nine months not drinking and I head back to Orkney. Worn down and scrubbed clean, like a pebble.
	I take the ferry and watch the waves crash into the boat.

Ghosts like gannets sweep along the sea.
I think of a selection of selves who have
crossed these shores. From the first, to now,
I think of them all.

I can feel myself trying to come back to
something but in truth – I have no idea what
I'm doing. What I am going to do. I thought
stopping would be the hardest part but being
well. And staying well – is so... boring.

The monotony of it... it feels like its own
type of poison.

DAD Cold out.

Storm tomorrow.

Managed to put my elbow through my
jumper.

He points at a hole in his jumper.

Your mother made me that.

*He sits. He concentrates on rolling a
cigarette and talks almost to himself.*

Long silence.

I'll sew it up tonight, the hole.

WOMAN I can do it.

DAD It will be lambing time before we know it.
Will you be here for it? The lambing?

WOMAN Depends on how the job applications go.

DAD Back to London, is it?

Long silence.

WOMAN The job centre called me.

I think their patience is running out.

DAD There's not many jobs on the island at this
time of year.

But you'll find something.

WOMAN   How did you know it was farming? How
              could you be so sure it's what you wanted
              to do.

DAD   It's just what I always wanted. And animals
              are so much easier than people.

WOMAN   Searching for a signal and smoking I listen
              to songs from London and look up photos
              of places I used to go. Counting the days
              since I left. Declining calls I cannot take.
              Because there are only so many ways you
              can say – sorry.

              I'm sorry. I'm sorry. I'm… and I can't stop
              thinking about drinking.

              Silence.

              Eventually I get a job working for the
              RSPB. In bird conservation. I count
              corncrakes. A rare bird, dwindling in
              numbers. Pink beaks. Brown with a ginger
              wing. Weighing only one hundred and fifty
              grams.

              The main reason for their decline is
              mechanised farming methods, as the
              mowers kill the chicks living in the grass.
              They travel all the way to Central Africa
              and back. To here.

              And so, I'm driving every back road on
              the islands of Orkney. Aching to hear their
              calls. In the dark. Sharing the night with
              cats and voles and hedgehogs and sheep.
              Both me and the corncrake cling onto our
              existence.

–   One breath.

              Two breaths.

              Three breaths.

WOMAN   And I'm asked to count the number of
          calls I hear from the male birds, I count the
          number of calls on my phone, counting on
          myself to get through this. I go out at night
          and listen. I go for nights without hearing
          one and then, in the darkness, I hear him.
          Calling out. Telling me I am not alone.

–   One breath.

          Two breaths.

          Three breaths.

WOMAN   Seven weeks – counting corncrakes,
          counting the number of days not drinking.
          And I can't remember the last time I
          laughed.

          The clock on the dashboard reads three a.m.
          and I'm out alone again.

          I stand outside to smoke. Look at the stars.

          And I feel so...

          I am so...

          And then.

          Out of nowhere. Just a few feet in front of
          me. A corncrake.

          There he is. Just a glimmer of him in my
          torch light.

          He looks as me, his eyes like beads.

          All feathers and freedom.

          You are alive.

          He confirms his own survival.

          We both do.

          You are alive.

–	One breath.
	Two breaths.
	Three breaths.
WOMAN	You are alive.
	Silence.
DAD	You're leaving?
WOMAN	Just for a little while. A season maybe.
DAD	I thought you'd go south, not further north.
WOMAN	I've been reading all about Papay. D'you know it's only a mile wide?
	Silence.
DAD	I've not been there in a long time. We went once, I think. When you were just a baby. How many people live on it now?
WOMAN	About ninety or so folk on it.
DAD	Ninety-one with you.
WOMAN	And a hundred and fifty different species of birds.
DAD	Amazing there is any room for humans.
WOMAN	It's the bird watcher's cottage I'll be staying in. They get folk like me to keep it occupied to ensure nothing happens to it.
DAD	The weather will be even more wild up there.
WOMAN	Will you be okay without me?
	DAD *laughs, just a little.*
DAD	I don't get a visitor from one week to the next. I'll be perfectly fine. It's me who should be asking will you be okay…

Do you think you will be…

Silence.

Will you get phone signal?

WOMAN   I don't even know if there is running water.

–   One breath.

Two breaths.

Three breaths.

WOMAN   On my way to plane, I look at pictures of London and begin to reread my diaries.

I am my only audience. And the expanse of that loneliness is…

–   One breath.

Two breaths.

Three breaths.

WOMAN   The flight over to Papay is the shortest domestic flight in the whole of the UK. You're only just up before you're going down.

–   You're only just up before you're going down.

You're only just up before you're going down.

You're only just up before you're going down.

WOMAN   The cottage is cold. And compact and I decide to live in one room, by the fire.

Taking life back to the bare bones. Because I have no idea what fucking else to do.

A phone call.

PERSON   How many days are you on?

WOMAN	Three hundred and twenty-three days without a drink. You?
PERSON	Nineteen.
	A few things happened and I just... the social worker got me a job volunteering in the charity shop. So, that'll help. Hopefully.
	Keep me out of trouble.
WOMAN	I'm sure it will.
PERSON	I was surprised when your number came up. You usually just message.
WOMAN	I just wanted to hear someone else's voice and I didn't know who else to... but I'm sorry, I know you've a lot going on and /
PERSON	You don't need to say sorry. Not to me.
	You're doing a good thing, staying off it. I wish I had your strength.
WOMAN	I don't feel strong. And it doesn't feel like it's getting any easier.
	I still – miss it.
	I know I'm not meant to say it and I know it's mad but...
	I miss it.
PERSON	Yeah.
	Me too.
	But I'm not letting it win.
	I am not letting it win.
–	One breath.
	Two breaths.
	Three breaths.

WOMAN   And when the weather allows, I walk and
               walk and walk.

               Returning. Repeating. Reliving. Refining.

               Reading my diaries.

               My mind replaying everything.

               It's just me. The coast. That cottage.

               So much space and I still feel so – trapped.
               By my own thoughts.

               I've forgotten how to live.

–   One breath.

               Two breaths.

               Three breaths.

               One breath.

               Two breaths.

               Three.

               One.

               Two.

               Three.

               One.

               Two.

               One. One. One.

SCIENTIST   Hello.

WOMAN   Fucking hell!

SCIENTIST   I'm sorry I really tried not to scare you.

WOMAN   Then you should have tried harder.

SCIENTIST   Yeah – sorry.

               I really didn't mean to /

WOMAN	You're the scientist. Investigating wave power.
SCIENTIST	Yeah.
	How did you /
WOMAN	Nothing stays a secret around here.
	Plus, it makes a change from all the archaeologists.
SCIENTIST	You're a local?
WOMAN	I guess.
SCIENTIST	Are you here for the sunset?
WOMAN	No... I'm writing.
SCIENTIST	Work?
WOMAN	It's a diary.
SCIENTIST	I didn't know anyone kept diaries still.
WOMAN	I do.
SCIENTIST	I brought some whiskey up to enjoy with the... light changing. Bloke at the wee shop said we might be able to see the northern lights tonight so I...
	He said it's delicious.
	Certainly expensive. Not that those two things are... well, you know. I'm just... I thought it be nice with the...
	Drink?
	Silence.
WOMAN	So. Are you leaving, or am I?
SCIENTIST	Excuse me?
WOMAN	There is a whole island here, plenty of room.
	So, are you leaving, or am I?

–   One breath.

Two breaths.

Three breaths.

WOMAN   I have a scar on my head, which I keep
catching myself touching. I find out my
attacker went on to attack another woman,
and he was found and arrested. I choose not
to attend the court case. He was sentenced
to six years for two counts of attempted
rape. Six. Years.

On Papay, one of the few things in excess is
time. So, I begin carrying out semi-scientific
experiments on myself. I download a period
app and watch my period sync with the
moon. I've been tracking my sleep cycles
and carrying out surveys of my dreams.
I am trying to expand into my environment
but...

–   Four hours of sleep.

A waning crescent moon.

Bleeding for five days.

Two dreams of drowning.

Three dreams of drinking.

One dream of Dad.

Hooded crows. Black guillemots.
Redshanks and oystercatchers.

And gulls.

And gulls.

And four hours of sleep.

A waning crescent moon.

Bleeding for five days.

Two dreams of drowning.

Three dreams of drinking.

One dream of Dad.

Hooded crows. Black guillemots.
Redshanks and oystercatchers.

And gulls.

And gulls.

WOMAN   I think about drinking again. I think about
               red wine with red meat. I think about sitting
               with a cold beer on the first day of summer.
               I think about mulled wine at Christmas.
               Fizz on birthdays. Vodkas in nightclubs.
               Whiskey when the weather turns.

               And I wonder how long is long enough and
               if I can ever just have one single /

SCIENTIST   The corncrake wife.

WOMAN   Excuse me?

SCIENTIST   That is what they call you.

WOMAN   Why is that we keep on bumping into each
               other?

SCIENTIST   Why do they call you that?

WOMAN   It's what I introduced myself as – when I
               worked to count and protect the corncrakes.
               They are /

SCIENTIST   I know what they are.

WOMAN   I used to visit farmers to try and get them to
               change their mowing patterns, help save the
               chicks.

SCIENTIST   And they did that?

WOMAN   No one ever flat-out refuses – that's not the
               Orcadian way. They just say they'll think
               about it, and I never hear from them again.

               Silence.

SCIENTIST	You're not very good at small talk, are you?
WOMAN	I don't really have time for it at the moment.
SCIENTIST	Too much to do?
WOMAN	I just don't find it very interesting.
SCIENTIST	Then tell me – why don't you drink?
WOMAN	Why do you ask?
SCIENTIST	Well. There is usually a story, isn't there? If someone doesn't drink.
	My dad was an alcoholic. He never kicked it though.
WOMAN	I'm sorry.
SCIENTIST	We all have our things.
WOMAN	No. We don't.
	Silence.
	Merry dancers.
SCIENTIST	What?
WOMAN	That's what we call the northern lights here. Merry dancers. You mentioned them the other day and I thought you should know.
SCIENTIST	I didn't end up seeing them in the end.
WOMAN	Tangles means seaweed. Muckle for big. Peedie for small.
	Where do you belong?
SCIENTIST	London. But I grew up in Glasgow.
WOMAN	Inland. Wet.
SCIENTIST	I suppose. When you put it like that. It certainly wasn't as wild.
	I just don't know how you do this... all this weather.

WOMAN	Most weeks I see more seals than people.
SCIENTIST	Sounds lonely.
WOMAN	I was just as lonely in London.
SCIENTIST	Do you think you'll go back?
WOMAN	I don't know what I'd be going back for...
SCIENTIST	London can be brutal, but I love it. All those lives just... can't imagine being anywhere else.

Silence.

WOMAN	Have you collected all the information you need?
SCIENTIST	Most of it. For now.

We still can't make something strong enough to withstand the waves. Well, something that's strong enough and economically sound.

Silence.

In truth, I'm looking forward to getting home. I leave next week.

WOMAN	I'll be here till spring.
SCIENTIST	I hope it becomes less lonely than London. I can't imagine dating up here if very – easy.
WOMAN	Truth is I can't imagine dating anyone.
SCIENTIST	Why?
WOMAN	Because I – can't – imagine dancing sober.

Because I can't...

Because I...

Silence.

SCIENTIST   Are you okay?

              Silence.

              Where are you going?

WOMAN   I climb and climb and climb unsteadily to
              the top of the trig point on North Hill. And I
              continue out to the cliffs of Fowl Flag. The
              most northern point. After that it's just...
              ocean.

–   Oceans.
              And earth.
              And ancient Gods.

              Oceans.
              And earth.
              And ancient...

              Oceans.
              And earth.
              And...

              Oceans.
              And...

              And...
              And...
              And...

WOMAN   And my heart is wild and open and empty.
              I've reached the edge.

              I howl as loudly as I can into the churning
              water, my cry is caught by the waves and
              blown back to the shore.

              I weep and wail at the waves.

              I weep and I run. Down to the water's edge.

              My feet pound on the ground.

–   And...
              And...
              And...

WOMAN   I stop on the shoreline. Inches away from crashing waves.

Undone and alone. Water and wounds.

I could walk right into that water, and no one would even…

And there, unearthing itself the glint of a glass bottle.

Washed up and waiting. The red cap of vodka.

Even the feeling of the glass in my hand is…

Two mouthfuls left in the bottle.

Enough to feel the burn, the buzz.

Enough to…

WOMAN *unscrews the cap and smells it.*

–   Returning. Repeating. Reliving. Refining.

Returning. Repeating. Reliving.

Returning. Repeating.

She drops the bottle.

WOMAN   And in that moment – I know. I know if I ever take another sip – I will die.

Not straight away. But slowly. Like a stone sinking to the bottom of the ocean. There will be no way to come back.

I've been trying to outrun the thought for weeks and weeks and… but it's followed me here to the edge of the earth.

And for first time ever, I see. Being sober isn't just for now.

It's forever. It's – for life.

–	I am stronger than… I am stronger than… I am… I am.
SCIENTIST	You make a strong coffee.
WOMAN	Sorry, there's no milk.
SCIENTIST	Oh, it's okay.
	Thank you. For taking me in.
WOMAN	You wouldn't have made it back to your place before the storm.
SCIENTIST	'Extremely vulnerable.'
WOMAN	What is?
SCIENTIST	Orkney. It's been classed as extremely vulnerable to climate change. Due to rising water levels, more rainfall…
WOMAN	It must be hard – knowing what you know.
SCIENTIST	Yeah.
	In all honesty… if I let it, it would make me fucking furious. But I don't let it. I can't.
	I need to believe people will and can change. Because if we don't…
WOMAN	Because if we don't change, it will kill us.
SCIENTIST	Well, yeah.
	Silence.
	Do you think you'll ever do anything with all your diaries? A book, maybe?
WOMAN	Maybe.
SCIENTIST	Do you think I'll be a character in it?
	Silence.
	Nah, didn't think so.

WOMAN	I used to want to be a journalist. I loved writing about art and glamour and gigs and…
SCIENTIST	So, what do you write now? Or maybe, the question is – why do you write now?
	Sorry. If that's too personal or /
WOMAN	No. It's just.
	I can't remember the last time someone asked me that.
SCIENTIST	It's probably a silly question to even /
WOMAN	I guess I write to… understand. To share.
SCIENTIST	To help?
WOMAN	Maybe.
SCIENTIST	Maybe, what we are doing isn't so different after all.
	We're both trying to capture something. Understand it. Use it – as power.
WOMAN	Or maybe, it's just habit.
SCIENTIST	Not a bad habit though, is it?
WOMAN	I wonder if it's time for new habits.
	Their hands briefly touch.
	Oh.
SCIENTIST	What?
WOMAN	No… it's just a relief. To…
	Their hands move closer.
	Silence.
	They move closer to kiss. But in the last moment – the WOMAN *pulls away.*
	Silence.
SCIENTIST	Oh, I'm sorry I /

WOMAN	No. Thank you.
	Thank you. Though.
SCIENTIST	I just /
WOMAN	You didn't do anything wrong.
	It's just – possibility is – enough.
	The possibility is…
–	Limbs and light. Ancient and animal.
WOMAN	The rush of red cheeks.
–	Limbs and light. Ancient and animal.
WOMAN	The shimmer of cold water.
	Tangles, limpets.
–	Limbs and light. Ancient and animal.
WOMAN	Deep breath. Closed eyes.
–	Oceans. And earth. And ancient Gods.
WOMAN	I want to live.
	Please.
	I want to…
	A rush. A hit. A high.
–	I am stronger than you. I am. I am. I am.
WOMAN	I feel free.
–	One minute.
	Two minutes.

Three.

Four.

Five.

Six.

WOMAN   I have never been so sure that I am alive.

And that feeling is… joy.

And I climb out.

To tepid tea and sandy towels.

I see now, my body has been hibernating.
Hiding. Healing. And above all – what I
need now is – joy.

An outdoor swimming club. Women,
mostly, not exclusively. But mostly.

And they don't ask me any questions
except about swimming. And I am so very
thankful. We are all here for one very
simple thing – to swim.

And now I try to do it every day – it's
not always nice. But it's always there
when I want to shock myself awake after
screens and central heating. Blast away the
frustrations. And I swim alone and with
friends. Friends. And I begin to write, again.
I write about swimming and recovery and…
life. A new life.

The waves have brought me back to myself.

Reminding me that it is not enough just to
be alive, but I must also /

DAD   How was she?

WOMAN   The lamb's arrived.

A female.

Both are healthy.

DAD	That's good. That's… early. Nearly two weeks.
	Two weeks early… just like you.
WOMAN	It made you ill.
	Me – arriving early – made you unwell.
DAD	Yes.
	I believe it did.
WOMAN	We've never talked about that.
DAD	No.
	But…
	Well…
	Silence.
WOMAN	Why don't we talk about it? All those times you were /
DAD	Nothing to say about them.
	I am not like you. I don't wish to tell stories.
WOMAN	Folk might find it interesting.
DAD	Aye, well maybe. But, no. Thank you.
	Not everyone has to… you know.
	There are plenty of better things to be – than interesting.
WOMAN	Yeah.
	Silence.
	I got that money by the way. That wee grant. It helps start putting my ideas together.
DAD	For the book? All your journals and that?
WOMAN	Yeah.

DAD	Been a long time coming.

Silence.

WOMAN	I – worry.
DAD	About what?
WOMAN	I don't want – everything – to be defined by…
DAD	Drinking?
WOMAN	Or the absence of it.

Silence.

DAD	No. But it will get easier.

Silence.

WOMAN	How do you know that?

Silence.

DAD	Things just tick on, don't they?

It will be lambing season again before we know it.

Silence.

And if you get it all down. Get it all out. Then you don't need to carry it about with you.

WOMAN	Who did you learn that from?
DAD	You.

Silence.

Now. I have a task for you.

There is a wall that needs mending. Near the Outrun. One of the stone ones. You'll need to break it down to rebuild it, but don't spend too long getting perfect. It won't ever be perfect; it just has to be strong enough for the storms. That's all.

Silence.

WOMAN   Thank you.

DAD   For what?

               DAD *smiles and leaves.*

               WOMAN *smiles. And, she continues onwards.*

               The End.

www.nickhernbooks.co.uk

facebook.com/nickhernbooks

twitter.com/nickhernbooks